FREE VERSE EDITIONS

Edited by Jon Thompson

FREE VERSE EDITIONS

Edited by Jon Thompson

2007

Child in the Road by Cindy Savett
Verge by Morgan Lucas Schuldt
The Flying House by Dawn-Michelle Baude

2006

Physis by Nicolas Pesque, translated by Cole Swensen
Puppet Wardrobe by Daniel Tiffany
These Beautiful Limits by Thomas Lisk
The Wash by Adam Clay

2005

A Map of Faring by Peter Riley
Signs Following by Ger Killeen
Winter Journey [Viaggio d'inverno] by Attilio Bertolucci, translated
    by Nicholas Benson

THE FLYING HOUSE

DAWN-MICHELLE BAUDE

Parlor Press
West Lafayette, Indiana
www.parlorpress.com

Parlor Press LLC, West Lafayette, Indiana 47906

Printed in the United States of America
S A N: 2 5 4 - 8 8 7 9

Library of Congress Cataloging-in-Publication Data

Baude, Dawn-Michelle, 1959-
  The flying house / Dawn-Michelle Baude.
      p. cm. -- (Free verse editions)
    ISBN 978-1-60235-054-0 (acid-free paper) -- ISBN 978-1-
60235-053-3 (pbk. : acid-free paper) -- ISBN 978-1-60235-
055-7 (Adobe eBook)
    I. Title.
    PS3602.A93F55 2008
    811'.6--dc22

                                        2008006449

Cover designed by David Blakesley.
Cover art: "Plant," 2008 by Curt Asker.
Cover background image: "Green grass and blue sky," © 2007
    by Narvikk. Used by permission.
Printed on acid-free paper.

Parlor Press, LLC is an independent publisher of scholarly and
trade titles in print and multimedia formats. This book is avail-
able in paper, cloth and Adobe eBook formats from Parlor Press
on the World Wide Web at http://www.parlorpress.com or
through online and brick-and-mortar bookstores. For submis-
sion information or to find out about Parlor Press publications,
write to Parlor Press, 816 Robinson St., West Lafayette, Indi-
ana, 47906, or e-mail editor@parlorpress.com.

for Alex

CONTENTS

ACKNOWLEDGMENTS

Grateful acknowledgment to the editors of the following pub-
lications where versions of some of these poems have appeared:
*Aufgabe, Big Sky, Derivations, Feschrift for Gustaf Sobin, Sans Issue,
Slope, Talisman, Traverse,* and *Verse.* I am also grateful to Skanky
Possum Press, who published an earlier version of *The Beirut
Poems* in a chapbook edition. I would also like to thank Joanne
Kyger, Alice Notley and Andrew Zawacki for encouraging this
manuscript; Anne-Shelton Aaron, for logistical assistance; and
especially Sally Fischer, for supporting this work.

THE FLYING HOUSE

FIELDWORK I

I was late, delayed

by a ground fog
a mistral, a heron
I found a piece
it was missing

clung to the rock
the displaced plain
I found a number of mirrors

undoubtedly paused, lingered
went about my collections
fingered an indentation
the nearly negligible curve of a bronze ring

a hawk arced overhead

found I was standing again just there
found myself
separating flint from flint
a history of gaps, disparity, lacunae,
though a rhythm could be heard

heard

moored
flush alongside
I detected letters in the profusion
a world of shadows

omissions

how else to know where we're going

I pluck, gather, salvage what I can

REMINISCENCE

LET US INCUBATE

(the) (forgotten)

let us remember
synapse gap
cleft
this is where
it fell
the toy the child
loved
the current
took it away

this is where

you don't look

step over

the chasm
the air of
the signature
seashell
animate, mirror
the point of the
arrow
by the wayside
dissolved signifiers

delicate parchment
    something dies from something
        far worse than it claims

    scattered artifacts
  lost nominals

a volatile wide-driven sediment
over the millennia
    the unraveling
      of the current itself?

    the jump
  into the void
      tastes of salt
        of burnt meat
          proteins forming

            these were
            messages
             we'd never
           understand
        forming
  loves
    lost fur

  the odd
button a freckle
  a tiny glass bead rolls
      off the edge

      and into

  there's a hand reading
hand
stroking

when one body
touches another
    exchange occurs
       the cellular
          the electrical
            I am an emotion
                charging

         see the trace of light in the air?

timed
        among impulses
    and potentials
           all that's ever
      wanted
    body against body

a tattoo

       a depth
   feels
    sustenance

      listening

POSTCARDS FROM IR)RATIONAL LANDS

1)

Had thought to write to you. Of the land where.

But the angles / at first / too (tight) (so restrained we / or I / some bearing / the pieces) the glass and the light.

I was given a lens. It darkened / "scry" (a vestige) worded the storm / nerves (spark) (melodic, a ringing).

Seeing better after sleep, image, so looks / lifts the air / curtain / but I am present / (counter) factual.

The ways of reason are too defensive for all tellings.

Here / I find… (my sense of) (nostalgia) (fashion) (so very slow).

Not to just forget because. Just not to.

This (feeling). Timed. That still.

2)

Gaze / Glaze.

I was caught by myselves.

Stranded. Desert /-ed (seas) (sand).

Where you would enjoy being, this sojourn / open to (unclear).

Would you risk / joining / the address is / some torn / flutters / so lovely, soft / a varied / transparency / some clear / through. I was not. Edged out.

Traumatized by the rational (ever in strange / climes I / thought) did not / think / you could (or could not) risk (ridiculous) (feel) (edge) (learn to) stop.

Look. Step forward.

Wipe the lens clean.

3)

The directions are (a sense of) (far) sea-faring (steer along) before the known (map) (courtesy) a speck of (life) light.

You would really love.

You would (souvenir).

Where (the directions) in tolerance. In distance (evidence) I want to (wanted to) refuse responsibilities in an age (disheveled) (skeptic) (splinter) (theories of language) speaks the other knowing.

Smell of salt (today I) (we saw) and then the long (so) (relaxing).

Just walking around not / too hot more / variable thin air (clouds).

Just like a (real) (so sit) feet in the water / not to think (feel).

4)

I could see over there (you too).

A form (or monument) of (power) (blessing) rapt this communication (more than lines).

The old windmill, arms flailing (once when) legacy (misplaced) / diamonds / sand / find stars / art (he said it was / a dream, sculpted / the wind) (water) strange as if memory (rivaled) reveal (find) after (before) to interrogate (let never / alone). More I felt.

Just by looking.

5)

These (incoherent) (luxuries).

So solved / the mystery (just plain wrong).

From dream to reality not identical paths (channel) canal (the dots). Some arrogance thought. Some did (silence).

I would egypt myself no other (word). Adventured. Fun. The sack cloth, presumed jewels.

To have visited (that) (place) / to let / out / stretched so / this note.

Wish you were here, too.

Waiting for (what) brings (turns) new / the ephemeral (softly moves).

A discourse of air.

6)

I, symbol.

Proof (mere perspective) vanish (now you see it) (that was what) the open / image / admits / human (yearns for) fill (full) / pulls the shutter (the danger of suns) radiating (invisible) light inside sees

References heaped (perhaps a new) / myth we made / our own / cell.

Wherein roars (the deep) night (dreams) sounds / could repel / city perhaps / but in (the rare) natural landscape (see postcard).

An echo of an old (forward) (idea) (evaporates).

I touched silky / recognized fur. There was nothing to lose. Now.

The slighted / knowledge of.

Taut over bone.

7)

Never to say alembic.

Thus / appearances / lend comfort (the perfumed) (easily dismiss) (experience) not our own.

Anyway it bubbled / topped / containment not / (answers) (echoes) the persistent (matter) what repeats (the value) a curve, a curved / toward an opening / (skies) put the lens / lights / what we / could / could not (prevaricate).

Some thought / not / exact / while (in here) (the heart) (hormones).

Whole vocabularies (shut) (tight ass). Another overlooking / a kind of (hope) / possible / eternity (sneeze).

I (for one) will visit again.

8)

Back here.

(Tourist) frequent / other / words.

Be honest (measured) (hoped) (slept) was waiting / hears / footsteps (door) (chasm) charismatic / a music / song of / bells. Toward an interior / I saw / spun / radiation / over & / flint.

Many restaurants, good shopping.

But for needs / a feeling / called (believed) exit / existed / some child cooed. Accepted. There is more than I could ever see.

Subjective (or subjected) / toward / the open(ings) (could it / be no one / noticed) (that was hardly) possible.

Needed those words.

I, too, was wrong about.

So slowly return (see you soon) (when).

FIELDWORK II

A trace, some vague

the barest of outlines eluded

between thumb and forefinger

on the threshold of antecedent

it justified fascination
it was water gushing in the forest
it was made of clay   of flint
carved in the impetus of passage
of ground
two wind-worn arches
the sight of a surviving outcrop,
surfeit of lavender, fresh
olives
at the fringe of the monuments
by the gardens of effigy and air

by the narrow stone bridge
where one walked one walks

it was rosettes and tendrils
it was propitiatory, ear upon the earth,
the ground the
curative incubations

          it hovered among prodigious volumes
               the existential necessities of fact

it was precise, partial, indistinct

             the eloquence of the void
   and misplaced source

bearing singular witness

        that its text still underlies our own

ONCE UPON A TRAIN STATION (A MUSEUM)

————————————————— I.

when in
Turino   (a sign)

Museum of the Shroud of Turin

(take) (a) (disastrous) (object)
why not, I
a narrative

mistaking the   subject
for the   subject

some Palestine in which / I / stood
Shabra, Chatilla
distant
scrim
the heat the
shapes
shadow,
the heaviest cast
lightly
stencil   what was laid

grave

great-great-great-great
remains

culture

the ruins, this a relic
history

some fundamentalism

devastates (acts

(action) some way

p- p-p ppppppp—

something sharp whizzes

(as is)   p-

st

——————————————————— II.

(perfectly) negative

positive

Secondo Pia almost

someone

almost

look out

dropped

a large photographic

look

pppplate

(the mirror)

this is an art

say the conservators
restoring (self) (portrait) see
the artist (they)
look (watch)
every apparently
the portrait looks   back

over

here!

across

                     the room
                                 centuries
                   a cross in question
                some millennial
                   symbol how curious
                   uncomfortable
                        the body embarrasses
                        the subject

Secondo (literal) went to the bar

                                        lawyer by trade
                                        in 1892 the one who

            the explosion

      flash goes the

(this is imagination)

                        dimensions I could never quite

                                          14' x 3'7" wide
                                          woven 3-to-1
      (a trilogy)
                          Syrian herringbone, a kind of twill

      (rhymes with)

did a fish just—

               here's the frontal, there's the dorsal
                           there the odd
                    topography of this clothe

everyone hangs at popular Rae's corner,
        lingers comfortably at Frie's patch

      see (the sign)

          of a
    (the hidden)
           marked

    puncture between

    what looks like
           capped, not crown

  hands (must, of course, be) crossed
           over the human

    and the thumbs—
         this is the stuff of war

(I've always felt)

language innocent

         image indelible

    fatal
    so say some

   of (what)   (what) used

   (no words)

         an enlightenment

    the belief

——————————————————————— III.

small colonies of hyphomycetes
rhomboid crystals of ara-
gonite
found only in limestone
these are cut
they say the living
rock
cools inside
the threshold of
where the Dead
Sea
waves (a gesture)
something afloat
thought it
floats

57 pollens

16 singular to

Palestine
called Palestine
consistent
the flax, a trace loomed
a deep vowel
doom
of cotton no European
this is really no paint
no mercury sulfide, no iron oxide
absolutely no susceptibility to solvents

p-p-p-p

make the damn thing go away

no doubt about orthogonal projection
apparent traces of the

sarcopoterium spinosum
hear the spine? something cracks
opens,
spin, floats, looms again

small amounts of strontium and iron
in the microscopic
earth,

always a very human heel

a total absence of ammoniacal gas
that means it was
quick, very quick

and so passed the VP-8 analyzer
microdensitometer tests
evident hematological immuno-
fluorescence x-ray
fluorescence porphyrin fluorescence
indicative microspectrophotometric transmission
positive hemochromogen,
cyanomethemoglobin
even bile detection

(Arian, at long last, retrieves his head)

and human corpuscles, human albumin
the image   on the surface
a microfibril
(or two

        the shadow
    seeps through
        the linen
           as life
                the story

       one life, and another, and
                   quite rationally
   a superficial image
(warned) us
           feared
  heard only

   human, what we say

    among selves,
        repeating keeps

    the story

——————————————— IV.

Fourteenth-century flummery

> remarked my learned
> father-in-law

confident, rigorous, skeptical
an admirable intellectual who

> history

my-my
> hysterical

I will not be

> literal

more a question of

> inquiry is healthy

how to even approach—

and the distinguished Hungarian Oboist
wandered to the look-out
where I, a cloud of birds,
their wings sharpening the air
(they're called *spatz* in German)
saying explanations
only satisfy
those who

> usually painting

later
the coma theory
the da Vinci theory

(dumb, he was born way after)

underestimates

> so overstating
> though Pierre Barbet
> experimented extensively
> to crucify

> begin cadaver

Sebastiano Rodante
     and a collection of casts, the crumbling plaster

Hermann Moedder
     actually suspended medical school volunteers
       by their wrists
       some scientists
their wives' faces

please, please, that's enough—

          an odd head
        try marble, wood, clay

   take a linen cloth and immerse it in

    are the herbs fresh? what mixture of oil—
soils, heat, darkness & light, sweat
   factor in humidity

            once upon a

plosive

              has to be some

    anatomically correct
     perfect in every forensic detail

          really it's not a

  more of an impress, almost a kind of scorch
    printed upon a hair

  the invisible ones
on the back
  a young child's hand
    that thin

some relic

                of evolution

an indication of things to come

what do you say

      some guy wrapped in an image

we know

      p-p-p-p—ppppppppp

            photographic

the admission   a negative

             just made of cloth

———————————————————— V.

                        for want of proof
            for this reason
                                    the disputation
                        of proof
            for this is The Scientific Method
                        for want
                                    of wealth
                  for reliable
                              this wealth
            for the public
    risky   even in 1350
                        filmed
            for TV   1973

                                    (snicker) (we will snicker)
        fooling seems funny

            permission to clip some threads

        hung by its popular corners

(shshshsh, the relic is sleeping in an ornate drum)

        will it ooze? sometimes they ooze

            wash your hands first, wear gloves

            cover your mouth, disinfect your—

                        for there was significant sterility
                              in the family of Virgins

            the metaphors collide, no collaborate, no-no,
                                          corroborate

                        and the Torino Firemen
        (…that crazy guy again with a knife)

the Torino Policemen

FLASH!

x-rayed, measured, weighed

patched by Poor Claire nuns, their fingers trembling
stigmata pouring, our heroes
heiros
for this is a kind of passion

in Chambery, real flames

thrice saved

(trilogy again)

put it out
lock it in

folded, unfolded, folded

in the lineage, over the line, run a finger

photo   perhaps   or poem or map
Edessa, Constantinople
Greece, France
various counsels, permissions, denials

for the decision-makers
at the top are

are not

convinced
by the decision
made
every decision

a question of (this is private)

access
　the obligatory Princess, a personal snip
another, her

(snicker)

beneath the microscope
upon the screen
for every icon
consistent peculiarities
a kind of template
bone, hair, eyes
the model of the model which
those features that image
prohibitions, publications
on a door in Great Britain
a rare codex in Budapest

(often reliable, the Oboist said)

a pilgrim badge fished from the Seine
dying crusaders, their testimony

memento mori

on this actual day
that face

in every church

every, every

for every

and you, too

for image

certainly was

saved

——————————————————— VI.

     (then) when the poets
  of crusades
    thought verse
    cognitive,
       a kind of
     virtual
       repository
    and thus
   repose
     his grave
      The Book of Chivalry
  did Geoffrey de Charny (b. circa 1359)
    wear shroud too?

        first verified owner

(this) (a) (poet)   author of
         lost
       his, or your, or my
   we use the word life
         in saving
      King Jean
         various accounts
          (lots of savings)
       what was (not) lost
           this war
            that

     Charny? that a charnel—
   carnal, or is it cardinal

   confused with a Templar (at the stake)
    flames
        a literal referent

    porte-oriflamme

the same name?

another war

medieval, always or,
ancient

(Agamemnon ever)

how is it
hormonal

sticks, stone, rock

but words never

I feel (a thought)

they do

La Roche
took the shroud to safety in 1418

and the poet's tiny granddaughter
Margaret

s'il vous plait

her responsibility huge

rendez-moi mon suaire

please give me my shroud back

I'll offer you two castles, a chunk of property
in Burgundy, a hoard of serfs

the narrative of exchange clarifies

a thumbprint smears
the parchment

contrary to modern thought
very difficult to write upon

you have to *wound* it

then Chambery
Piedmont, and the

(what?)

Holy See!

RORSCHACHS ALL

(this is a test)

is that the wild tamarisk of Palestine? of the Anatolian Steppe?

among the cedar, a trace of pine, of pistachio
what variety of hazelnut tucked in the folds?

is that an eagle impressed on the coin of the eye?

(who, after all, sees an eagle)

what ties the hair at the back of the head?

are those really marks of a

that a shoulder bruised and

tibepoiy kaizaroz

hmmmm, such a strong, wide chest

where the trace of myrrh, aloe,

could be miso
(another continent)

not to be overly reverent
difficult to detach

the associations smoother the words

dare I risk frankincense?

what do you see in this

the shepherd's crook
can you even see it?

(change the negative to a

difficult to disentangle
from stain
tear and patch
a bizarre image
in any case

don't talk about it

vertical and horizontal
blood flows,
most everyone agrees

whatever that is

the earth is flat

evidence of final
orthostatic collapse

and lo—
in the sky

EXPLOSION

fragments sent to the Anglos
equipment sent to Italy

how can they
how (arranged)
(rearranged) who
Los Alamos National Scientific Laboratory

(an interrogative pronoun may require subject inversion)
right
something's not quite
nuclear physicists
thermal chemists
optical physicists
crystallographers
sudarium? chi è esso?
biophysicists
spectroscopocists
forensic pathologists
industrial radiographologists

(an interrogative personality may require
inversion)

not TOEFL, more moral
thought foreign
a language
as a global
meaning
industrial

the service
will follow
the opening
ceremony
as the sample
assessed
carefully
protecting
the double
blind study
results in
bound
incoming

(an inflected person may not follow orders)

THE DEFENSE INDUSTRY

IS ON THE OFFENSIVE

the Jet Propulsion Laboratory, the Air Force Weapons Laboratory
Sandia Scientific Laboratories, Hercules Aerospace Division
Cambridge, Yale, Harvard, MIT
the Spatial Data Analysis Laboratory of Virginia Tech

p‑p‑p‑p   p‑p‑p‑p

and there was mystery
in the carbon-dating protocol

(an infected shroud may imitate a shroud)

it is a thorny issue

again the blood
a stain perhaps
this use of force
natural, what we say is

fundamental

the strong, the weak

the electromagnetic
gravitational
embodied in the brain

a sensitivity to light
some kind of flash
flesh   war after war after
the explosion
cinders, ash
the clouds shrouded

made
fission
the image
of explosion
explain
again
and again

my how you struggle
make it go away
trans
substantiated
against   fusion
the facts
that word again

translated

meaning

just a piece of expensive linen
a kind of tablecloth

backed by holy

Canons

———————————————————— ∞

what is meant by   matter

bombarded by
neurons
isolating the isotopes
proposing a kind of
neutron capture
moderately strong x-rays
absorb sodium, silicon
phosphorus &c
admitting the secondary
(these are stronger)
something about
wavelength
overcoming the pions
dematerialization
associated spontaneous
decay
subatomically
the omission of
in the structure
of structure
a kind of
coronal
photo
particles
free
electrons
ionized
high energy
bright
very bright
(neurons again)
the emission
imperceptibly

                rapid
            the image
        superficial and
highly resolved
            this is really
                great chemically
                            physically
                but in theory

                    biologically
                the behavior
            of the body
            no reason
        radiates
    this way

[Stolen] (Remains)

I.

every (where
relics
the past
lists left
found shard, a kind of scraper
this digging, pulls
furs
the far
the tiny, tiniest
piece of wood, the willed
her of shape
hints womb
the found
shell, his skin
remains memory
in that
I
a memory
(family)
(origin)
the artifact
evidential
are
used, were
kept in
in pieces
the context
of ages
the reliquary

            fingers
    hands us
        what was lost
    hid
        the loss
    bit by
    bit

II.

of the
movement
(time)
(essence)
to sense
emotion
as in
curious
heard
(censored)
moves me
a sense
(this is
subjective)
I am
thus
caused
in pieces
these relics
found
windows
a scene
through
glass
the motion
heard
broken
glass
heard
(thought) (feel)
intention
some sensory
pattern

breaking

III.

                              the literal
                        object
                         a relic
                  (put) (aside)
                       translate
                  bones of
                       some
                  knows (knowing)
                       words
                        or vocables
                    relic it
                      (all) experience
            the ash
                     and bone
                       divides
            antique
                   from ancient
                     a feeling
                     keeps
                   hair even
                  blood
                      keeps
                     (knows)
                        see it
                   pours
                     literally
            some
                       inner
                  the interior

(looking) (glass)
it was
primitive
the church
alter the
sounding

(bomb)

heard bell

IV.

at
St. Marie-le-Mer
for memory
places
a church
where a source
translate spring
polished rock
translate box
the bones
translate belief
down to the sea
an archaic word
costumed
finery
two Maries times
three
I heard
caravan
translate gypsy
small boy, a crab
and flamingo, white
horse
bulls for the
arena
hear aria
the Maries
of memory
her hair

to her knees
some hand-tatted
lace
the veins
in her hands
a man
his tears
his Maries
translate
is the
word for
any place
real

V.

in Lumières
a man
hearing American
accent said
how do they
the beautiful, strange
lights
those rocks
up, up, the mountain
at night

it's dark
we say
protected
no one
even hunters
this time
of year
the cypress, oak
a few boars
fox
even a wolf
eagles, hawk
you
are mistaken

his nervous
laugh
later

I
the village
called Lumières
woke up
looked out
under stars,
waited

VI.

air
something
to do with
invisible
needed
a word
ravished
by rhetoric
internal
(heard infernal)
some official
calls indulgences
a word for taking
for taking for
granted
the sky
its rotation
its shroud
essentialized
in the name of
the war
no word
is ever

stop

worthy

stop

(the clouds)

of that

VII.

(remind us)

the memory
forgot
the emotion
in motion
for
get
a memory
more he
few her
motioned
(this is
forward)
the ex-
plosion
a suffix
reduplicated
among the particles
so very
in impossible
micro
heard shouting
there was
shouting
did you
hear
there were
words
exploding

VIII.

bits of bone
a thigh
a thin
wafer
of finger
the tiniest
fragment
of rib
mere dust
encased
the window
a tooth
a nail
the *furta*
sacra
heads
hands
at night
the bones
pull
part
the organ
deep
deeper
sounds
a body
scattered
in these
are scattered

a perfect match
and so identity
is put
the name
of the dead
I missed
so many
the odd
remnant
 some relic
this world
words left

IX.

stolen

               what was called

                              (the) (words) the

poet says (are) (missing)

              a feeling had

                    thought emotion

    every thought

              emotion

  some kind of destruction

                       of apocalyptic proportions

      who could have thought

         a book

                            Book

              something died in us

    look inside

                the fragments

         tell us

X.

and yet

      fine, fine earth
         thought green

     as if habit
or
 expectation where
           gardens
     jasmin and
       drums
         amid the counting
          it was sharp
              the deepest green
           feathers
        a light
      breeze
    a turning toward
   an orientation
a way of looking
  sound of wings

     flames again

         then the rain
            and the counting
          now how many
               the many

   the walls yet hold

     they kept

      keep on coming

Fieldwork III

Beyond the garden   the tablet

an accident

uncovered   at the edge   the narrow

abandoned worksite   signatures on the verge
of plentitude
          of irrecouperable

witness   space between spaces

          excavated lines
some spare misfortune at the extremity
          of provenance   accumulations,

signs of the imminent
                    ruins   what we've inherited—

meandering depictions   odd metaphors,
on the flickering screens
          of the unconscious self
                    thin and liminal

          at the limit

     of culture
                    at the vanishing
          entry of evidence

particles of breath
         of sound

    in the movement of rendered air

the sky's reflection   dissolves

    across   the very waters before me

    fragile   provisional   the being

between reeds and rushes
    a gradient far too slight for our own
  senses to appreciate
    drawn now   out of all

inherent context

    inadmissible

    the wish, to enter at long last the totality

of the given instant:

a present

itself

THE BEIRUT POEMS

I.

In the saw-tooth sky

explosive

plane engine   edgy helicopter pricked
a fistful of antennas
          even the darkest of spaces
                    ears, eyes
               fissured dishes upturned
          the roves are littered with surveillance
          with links, my love,

why not take advantage   of the motion
                    cast your lines

     into the emptiness   features

length
     the helicopter sieve of air,

          in the puncture, enraptured, be fumigated

          rants an arc   upset rover, river,
     modules sickeningly sweet
                    the red

                              shifts distant

     noises deafening
feelings

chipped among the cumulus
                            faulty embroidery
thread watcher
          trickles down my leg
                                 I'm done for
               eyeless fish, stunned star

festering at the seams no limit

                         this expansion

          a shelled loss

gusts then grieves

II.

And then the halt of a silence
and then planes razored the coast

something was cut—
it was a memory
here where the burden (time)
stratifies in rock.

Open it up
a fish fossils out   a skeleton
inscriptions from that primer
the one with ridiculous lessons
our boundary is indoctrinated
as number
as rules of etiquette

this is where / you sit / at the table

sample the *mezza*   all 56 dishes,
tiny roasted birds specific green fruits,
the women may eat   after
the men   later   when it's over   alone.

Explosions, bones.

They hammered the air
again someone we knew
just died

what comes with the dark
in the absence
a serenade of teeth
continuous analysis
forlorn   scream
another blast.

Later the TV
starts up again   connections

put back   in place   this is terrifying

efficiency
this is the way we do it

here   it's normal   information,

what might have really happened
if we'd paid more attention

again those bursts

I still run in my dreams.

III.

Out of my arms endlessly rocking

still the night / not yet warm
              separation   the least of love's
    desires   my hand and my other hand

and you chose   everything, they say,
            your fault or victory the dove whispers

                          frail receptacle

      anyone's ear   voice

    of chromosomes lettered   in algae, furry, grunts
    the labor of reading—

          testimonies, the old testaments, pink
      beneath the crust
         a kind of vapor
       my ceaseless wishing,

          the dollhouse
  splintered in the accident long ago

    the lap full

        weight of cell
                division,
          something / holds back
       strains

at the moment   marches a mommy
                    child

          we are a photograph   a letter before the pointers
          scriveners, recorder

old sequence of Ferris wheel   and cardboard   home

          safe in the war zone   slide over
                                                        down
                                              slips

                        body out of body

     an ocean washes
                    flows through the toxic
                              clicks /
          onto the next   forgive   and forgive

it must be selfish
                    a wont of humanity

          exploding

                    can't run now
                                   don't be scared

          it's just an emotion, like any other
     flows
                    through the appointed time

     leaves
                    an image

                    a phantom upon the face.

IV.

Caught behind the podium

I can't

I will not evade   this is my lecture

the veiled girls do not care for Allen Ginsberg

no one knows Kerouac
here they make unaffectionate reference

again Wordsworth, Eliot, always Arnold.

when will the promises
the highway, say, the one
without epic potholes, be completed?

Stranded on concrete blocks
next to the sea, all the artifacts stolen
even the abstractions

perform
without the asset of image
that of love   of pain.

Who could discuss poetry in this
ruckus   please
translate
shouting

a loudspeaker

the eruptions of bombs somewhere

I can bring you a difference
in pronouns
but I can't get you
work in this wasted economy
can't remove the dread
the polluted air

vegetables no one dare eat

shoe-shiners
not shoe-shiners

ears
to governments
with conflicting aims.

The precious, saccharine love
these students
revere
their mothers
culturally admirable perhaps
but the homeland
something else

mountains slapped by a soiled sea

the grapes must be peeled one by one
fallen skins left for a bird with trilled song,
a common species, they say,
able to survive wholesale ecologic disaster.

These young men
never had a chance to read
without a censor

but they're certain
Rushdie's a fraud.

Ideas I took

for granted are
like the clouds,

dangerous
and the fact that Ginsberg

is a Jew never seemed so important.

V.

Because the wheelbarrow is red

                because of bandages, red and white,
         culture of course
      in the wheel
            and chickens are, by nature,
                        nature,
         a tool is a tool
      because red and white
                sky America
          the icebox is stained
       bloody plums
             forgive us,
               Flossie, for screaming in the streets,
           so far from the farm
                  my ebony spinster, my rose
           the rain glazes
        the object that's attractive
      but a friend is in excruciating pain
                  where the good doctor
        applies image to a wound
                  no medicine can ever
      heal.
We could
                act like there's nothing wrong
      it's more dignified
     easier in rural
         America
             than here where boundaries

                         disintegrate with each
                            porous blast.

Everyone
    looks out the window when

        the explosion   when the explosion

        when the explosion. The words, apparently, don't

          exist

                  other things do, and we're afraid.

VI.

And those things fell out of the
sky

all night long

sad repetitive narratives,
one side against another side against

all sides

facets of distortion rob
us of light.

Will Nayla risk candles?
Will Alex have heat?

And the computer
sends a violent surge,
doubtless good-bye.

All the babies are crying in the dark—
but they're from the other side

the one we don't know about

can't find
on the spell-check.

It'll be harder buying
bread from now on, identity tags

at a distance   hair

                too light

            for these parts these are not sound

                    effects

          wars
                 American movies
                      made real. He watched them, too,
        that young man

        proud of innovation

      impossibly shiny

                  his slender rifle
             its silver
                   vaunts the moon

           rattles the stars,
 glints
    a knife   another
                  sacrifice, the sheep strains, stains
            the doorstep

                    smells of fresh
     death,
           any living, woman's or child's or man's

         hands full of a resolution
         you never then know

   you do have.

VII.

And the flood
olive groves   mountains
cracked in anger, time made the bird
made the sky widen,
literally, rocks,
no more literal than that, can Chicken Little
really be saved?   So little grass.

And the Dead Sea (lost) (even) (its waves).

There is no formal way out.
The caves
in the hillside don't connect, and
the roads   especially the recent ones, stop
at the border where the feast
of Cana
is recorded in stone near the place
of slaughter

banked in black
iris really the deepest blue

that season is past and the miraculous lake
the two men walked across mirrors

a distance

impossible   to entertain prodigies in this

unctuous heat.

It strangles the light.
There was no breathing.

The dead did not return.

A dusty sheep,

slips over the far dune, astray.

VIII.

The butcher   (missing three digits)
chops lamb, slices beef, greets

old friend   in my grey suit
(needs ironing)   and the veiled woman

peeks around the corner
she does not look Muslim.

If my own pagan heart
burned thyme, would the bad spirits

go away? The engines fly
over
head   leave us
alone

so alone, my shoulders
cold, all the roves in the city

won't stop this vicious

desert rain

won't drive the humidity away
the occluded air

no street lamps, light,
no electricity, not here in this

                                    some kind of nervous
fraying.
          Why have you come here? they ask—

                    the sidewalks, you know, are broken up,
          no one drinks wine

(we are weary)
                    deprived of providence, some song.

     It takes more effort than you

     imagine   we don't want any more trouble

          daddy hasn't come home yet, daddy
                    shot to death in 1982.

                                    Is it true?
                    Muslim women are experts in sex?

Confess: I love you more than anything sometimes
I won't show it.

In the sky patterns of error rush

     past the speed of sound, shattering
               windows
nerves, rustle the veils
               thousands, always interfering
                    thoughts to smoother feelings, would

          that I were nearer my mouth

                    you, too.

IX.

A blue or rose
view of antiquity
impossible, perhaps,

to decipher this odd
air,
the arabesque of migratory birds
announces a sharp
veer to the
left, and again
new scenery on a rotating earth

are you able, really able
to be here, now, out
of all regret?

The prayer song starts, rattles
the hovering
the part set in history,
the part

the wrong words held, slip,

reflect
there the part of me I told.

Still I can make out the form of

the temple   darkening sky,

view that keeps me so much
                    traveled, cities to camel, heady
          scent of gardenia, cedar, see

          hips quiver   artifacts under your chair

          I want only to understand

                              the lost cities

                    the broken mosaic

          the 78th name of some god

               a word never spoken with fish

are you reading?

     receiving?   A strange legacy pulses in
          the blood and the blue eye
from these parts, the one hung around the neck,

                    in the window

          wishes you well
                         but there's
               no resolution to the restlessness of time.

          Even now it pushes you

          into the street

strangers

               wonder

                    too at your

     being here.

SHUBAD

I.

thicken
(the air)
words
(thicken) (air)

ash

this strange (air)

tastes, you'd say

the distance

temporal
parchment
transparent fleck
what chemical
gold
leaf

spark
an aging sun

though representation
by nature
forbidden
(thought
impossible)
mere echo

a trace
    original leaves
      upon the skies

          some sort of modernism

   who says 'filigree'?

        says 'memory'

   entombed

      the exhumed ideas

   among (always) (those) bones

  (Rumi disagrees)

glints again, embered
  a book we

      and the work on stars & numbers
    water
     a particular plant
         how helps
       those to breathe easily
      those who could
       could not
        (coughs) (smoke)
       blacken the marble

   I shall graffiti a name

      and in the beginning

      and beginning in

      (time's error)

1) an old woman in cotton nightgown,
 watering white azaleas

2) a young man, his voice quivering,
describing one of the 7 Wonders
of the World

3) a notebook with a childish cover

4)

        another piece

    another

       the clouds

          other

   bruised flesh

        odd stains

               (it won't go out)

         strains

(a flute)

    rudely hums a tune

        our eyes

           sear

              the images
                (untidy)

              glints again
                there it is (hurry)

(Gap jeans in a fire truck)

And Hammurabi, skeletal, in

origin
private property
a series of triangles
stamped in clay

stray ingots dropped
in haste

content excised, and so rapidly intent

(a man weeps)

have you heard

Zenoubia?

(the present world)

the temple lintels
royal sleigh?

(the jaw slams shut)

away goes speech
the book
furious manuscripts, some
displaced
replaced
thoughts, a pen

what were words

over a sacrifice

something they must have said

II.

shshshshshsh

          don't speak

they will

     take voice

        (take) (your) (voice)

   shshshsh

   shshshshs

      they want you to be

           (quiet)

       (perfectly quiet)

your voice

     it's the (still) (sound)

   dull
    air

a trilled light
upon the silvered mirror

reflection (this censured)

your footsteps,

iris,
breathing

every sound

even the inside

the intimate

honey
click

in the child's throat

(distant)

(whisper)

your inner

letters

the code

beat   heart beat

the files so thick
the papers fall from

sky

rare
birds,

endangered

books

every course
teacher

(protect the teachers)

the fine scrim
of an idea

our ideas

(the) (words) (are)

sound

(you) (remember)

that sound

(recollection is dangerous)

the browser halts
the photograph

drifts from the screen
(no) (voice)

Hester, wordless,
and her wild daughter, watching

shshshshshsh

the place of first permission

a fragile meadow

fills with boundary

(take) (the vow) (of) (silence)

the robes of uniform
the tiny window

not even the open
opens fully

the vistas of democracy

barbed wire

the history
of barbed wire

shshshshs

we speak in one voice

shshshshsh

someone is still whispering

LUBERON DIALOGUE

(Looking up)

"What is the right word?"

For the faces of sky
(no words)
we have not produced

the correct sounds for feeling,
swimming in our throat,
swamped

What calls
the stone glows
yellow or pink or red
pivots away from
the sun
calls cheek or elbow, my
hope
is biologic, grows every night a
little taller
clouds float
out
our mouths

(answer) (caress)
answer   a number greater than the trine
of light when gravity (define) (gravity)

and when
"the feather is more than a feather?"
"How" (this question then heard) "a flower dies?"

Here is the arbitrary
called servitude, call lace ruffle or
bustier (something tightens)
(closes)
firmly (around) the throat

Wherefore
that emptiness sagging between heartbeats, quarter beats,
the full rhythm of desire, where desire, inner
to fill (fill)

wherefore fullness, wherefore "I put my head on his shoulder"

(where the I is) the you
surely

answers

a pronoun (with) (many) (names)
(the answer is traditionally poetic)

"tunnel" "passage" "poetic"

What means star really a star in your eyes that distance

photon emitted
sun?

Fire?

"What fire?"

flares
emotion, a word, a word for, what "are" "words" "for"?

"Why skin tears?"
say: edginess

necessary
    cuts perhaps, ideology, separate bone & muscle
        an answer
    (tissue thin)
a membrane of messages

        (synapse)

(chasm)

        Where?
    "lovely"

        "memory"

    should"

        "be"

(Heard then) ("How")

    "explain" (to him) "microscope"?
        closer
                say "a seed" the cherry (sheds)
            blossoms
                a luscious, delicate fruit
                a red reddens, a thorn

    What then does it mean—

                listen: listen the evening sounds
                blue line of blood bereft of
                    oxygen
                        the horizon

                respires the sky

    What is substantive

(in answer a noun)
is rational
& consequent

an opening where babies come from

(no replies)
the slow cessation & resumption of wave,
the sigh of knowing, hiss in the night, reflects image or orifice
particle moon

answers
faint cursive
a mesh of woollen,
those threads
spun from

"What are the threads spun from?"

Why insist
(evidence)
celebrate (continual loss)

"Why the 'a' the 'e'"?

when a life form
so small
the presence detected   (by)
disbelief
(finite)

lines

chemistry the alphabet to electrical impulse
(then) (understand)

a cricket in the knee
Appears Knee

answer an expectation parting lips
called "feelings"

"why love" brings relief

"Why is bleach noxious"

What makes that noise "just" "then"

answer a rule to a game you answer
with which aspect of the verb to play?

The answer was never in
facts substantive
heard incipient
a kind of civilization
effortless spreads

"Why do cells eat?"

(and blushing feels so silly)

"And death? (And after no answer) "Why water

("answered

(A paradigm deposits dust in the bed)

Is dust literal?
moisture settles on the glass, lips
upon the rim
an edge
get used to

"Why illness, egg, rock"

so lightly
strokes the

inner

arm

reply was "please me"

(there were candles)

Kaleidoscope. Doily.

"What sound the shutter"

closing after midnight
when bodies
buoy
dream

"What is" (your) (dream)

and the question (true)?

"What?"
"What" (the curtain)

a slice
translucent usefulness through
to a dimension
(mind)

(the)

answer no longer delayed

answers a verb another poet used

answer continuously answer a child's

the answer head-up

a smaller, more emotional (version) of (you)

FIELDWORK IV

Left, as ever, with what remains

"language"
"existence"   "the animate "
"the inanimate"

endowing each
with signs   countersigns
the marks
we need to know as we know

as the Rhone flows   overflows
the contours   wandering over
the broken ground
sculpted shells

some foreign object rises under the trellises
the damp   the reciprocal
imprints & amalgams
fingertips upon the nacreous lip
on the most intimate of skins
particulars in all their finery

something dropped   wine
was it water   upon the copper plate
a kind of calligraphy   keepsake,
a very particular kind of key

of whatever the future holds
anonymous data   the irrefutable fact

consciousness admits no severance

no "after" this

"life" alone

THE FLYING HOUSE
OF LORENTO

Up there!

it skies
scries—

really, my dear Lorento,
still
moving again
please, for once

stays curiosity
was it / curiosity
between lift off and

put down that box
(squared)
what is the number
(to) (build) (on)
space times emotion
I had trouble
reading
a word like formula
found (missing) foundation
some (tradition)
meaning memory
made / of real / stone

sudden, as if

the air speed the

a kind of translation

measured, the distance
fought among the calculations
and the port

a portal, pages
multiply
times (again) unexpected
lifts with
(the sentence)
up the chin, the neck stretches
squint, the eyes (pronominal / already possessive)
sees the house, mortared, stone by stone

flying

oh Lorento, we are
doomed
it can't be
matter moving

our own

material
neuronal
disposition
I could never
remember
empirical
heard etymology
(the relics)
epistemology
a kind of seeing / being
built upon the
common ground
lands
flies / skies again

witnesses

a shepherd, the shepherds
a hermit, the hermits
stocked among the narratives

in history
here, in this village, a shepherd
a hermit
still in history
we are, aren't we
and the
but this story, my Lorento, all my world

with a thump

stops (a difficult fit)

edgy, isn't it edgy
half in the field
half on their road

the door (always open) to the north
the window to the west

sets the sun

a word (the poet says) disappears from the poem

here, please come here

some word carries a box
lifts off

come back here right now!

the world is slipping

30 kilometres a second, I believe

my life is
come back here right this instant

and so belief

facts
coins, a couple of sculptures
these are the normal
relics
my subject
what we don't
dismiss
the mighty
listen, to entertain itself
a kind of knowing

smile (back again)

O Flying House of Lorento

please let's stay put!

(sound of bells)

have to hold it down
he brings his tools

books, maybe, give weight

just another piece of architecture
to shelter
this thought

was it secular?

space bends, even bows

gravity denies heresy

just stay still

encased
in decorative marble, inside
the basilica now

someone lived in this house
once upon a

we are not that gullible

proves fallible

am I

O Lorento

are we?

FIELDWORK V

To decipher the remains, say

of rock, or mouth, or absence of mouth
to gaze
in the wedge of the inarticulate page
to draw a pattern
a pattern across the water
filling the vessel with a vessel
water with luminosity
to bury
the thunder in an ancient rite
limestone rough cast from the quarry
to speculate on translation
on ceremony,
on a patch of earth
identifying this topography as forgotten
Aeria   Cella
the cratered outlines, the jagged shelves, to lift a char
from an imaginary fire
limpid light within the sheath
to body cognition in sentient debris
words   burials   journeys,
to orient the resonant fields of association
rhetorics   of shards & rhythm & strata

constituting an artifact, its own, a document

in perpetual process and acts of formation,
to let the circle predominate

the fluent   the continuous

no matter how deep

how very   high   overhead

NOTES

The title of this collection, *The Flying House*, is literal. In the ten years the poems span, from 1996 – 2006, I traveled on four continents and made homes of varying lengths in Paris, Brussels, Lacoste, New York, Beirut, Chicago, Goult, Alexandria (Egypt), Menerbes, and Luxor. My itinerary was driven, in part, by economic necessity; but it was also fueled by an intense desire to know the world, to experience its contemporary manifestations and to physically examine its historical remnants. And to render this experience in a poem.

My poems are "site-specific," more than anything else. By this I mean that I assume physical contact and virtual contact are dramatically different experiences. While on the surface, this distinction may appear self-evident to some readers, in practice it is difficult to satisfactorily explain, both in terms of philosophy and in terms of cognition.

At the core of site-specific writing is the idea that presence—of the writer, of the word, and of the subject—is intrinsic to a work of art. The ontological catalyst of the "site-specific" is taken for granted in the visual arts, but its usage in literature is more restricted, particularly in the wake of *fin-de-siècle* theories privileging absence. Since even my sense of "absence" is ineluctably "present," so to speak, I had to look elsewhere, far from the theoretical discourse that dominated the Bay Area of my youth. Over time, the act of writing became for me an historical "site," related in some ways to Susan Howe's notion of the "narrative in non-narrative." Actual details, conditions and circumstances litter the poems with a story of their making.

The "Fieldwork" series, which structures the book, was written in Provence, France, where Neolithic artifacts are plentiful to a trained eye. Gustaf Sobin needs to be mentioned here, because he knew more of this terrain than I ever will, and he taught me to pay attention to the wonder literally underfoot in an area known only modestly for its archeology. His book, *Luminous Debris*, speaks directly in this series. The site in "Fieldwork" is vertical, often reaching through time to a distant past when early man made a temporary home in the river valleys of southern France.

"The Beirut Poems" are more raw and immediate, written during a tense phase in Lebanese history, and "Once Upon A Train Station (A Museum)," takes impetus from a visit to Italy, where, on the way back to the train station in Turin, I happened upon a strange, naïve museum devoted to the Shroud of Turin. "[Stolen] (Remains)" furthers the investigation into the poetics and politics of relics, focusing on those I found around me when, upon another return to France from the Middle East, I found myself living in a portion of the Chateau of Babylon near the peak of Jerusalem down the road from the church where Jesus' Grandmother's bones are currently venerated. "Shubad" returns to the Middle East, to sites I visited in Syria and Jordan, and wanted to visit, in Iraq. Robert Duncan is in that poem and, I fear, throughout the book, since his classroom is among the most vivid sites I have ever experienced.

The inner frame of the book, the "Postcard" series and "The Luberon Dialogue," shift emphasis from the material site to the dialogic site of language, locating the writing self in and through the reverberating field of words where many poets speak. The Catalonian photographer, Israel Arsino, whose exhibition I saw in Saignon (France), lent inspiration to the "Postcard" series, while my son Alex's and my repartee in the Luberon is recorded in the "Dialogue." "Reminiscence" was written along the bank of the Sorgue in the village where Petrarch expatriated, and lastly, the title poem, "The Flying House of Lorento," offers commentary on a literal house that was said to fly, UFO-style, through the skies of the Middle Ages. Since this house carries the name "Lorento," it was easy to assimilate to the name of Laurent, who was my beloved companion during the peripatetic years that these poems were written.

Throughout my travels—both in language and in the world—I have struggled to find meaning that is more than sum of the conditions of its production. I am still looking.

—Rome, 2008

ABOUT THE AUTHOR

Dawn-Michelle Baude took the advice of her mentor, the poet Robert Duncan, literally: learn as much as possible about language and the world, and apply that knowledge to your writing. While studying with Duncan at the legendary New College of California, she wrote reviews (under the name of Dawn Kolokithas) of modernist and postmodern poetry for *Poetry Flash, American Book Review* and the *San Francisco Chronicle.* Her first books and chapbooks began to appear, including *The Tropologue* (Poltroon Press, 1986), a prose-poem memoir about overlanding in Africa, and *Notes for a New Theory of Pasta* (1987), a poetry spoof. In 1988-1989, she was appointed Assistant Director of the San Francisco State Poetry Center and earned an MFA in Fiction from Mills College. Then she left for Europe and the Middle East. Living mostly in France, Lebanon and Egypt, with extensive travel in Greece and Syria, she worked as a professional writer for Conde Nast, among others, publishing articles in *Vogue, New Woman,* and *Glamour.* She also published a steady stream of art criticism in *Art and Auction,* as well as chapbooks and fine press editions with small European presses, including *Gaffiot Exquis* (Arkadin, 1997) and *The Book of One Hand* (Liancourt Press, 1998). Collaborative and ghostwritten works from this period include the international bestseller, *Savoir Dire Non* (with Marie Haddou, Flammarion 1996, reprint 2006). During the 1990s, she also wrote a monograph on the Swedish artist, *Reconnaître: Curt Asker* (Réunion des Musées Nationaux, 2000) and earned a *Diplôme des etudes approndis* in Shakespeare from the Sorbonne. In 2000-2003, she returned briefly to the U.S. to get her PhD in English from the University of Illinois – Chicago, when *The Beirut Poems* (Skanky Possom, 2001) and *Egypt* (Post-Apollo Press, 2002) appeared. Upon returning to Europe, she joined the permanent staff in Comparative Literature at the American University of Paris, and in 2005, she received a Fulbright Award in Poetry that took her to Alexandria, Egypt. Her chapbook, *Through a Membrane / Clouds,* was published by Gong Press in 2006. In 2007, she taught in Rome, Italy, before returning to the U.S. She is guest editor of the 2008 edition of the international arts magazine, *Van Gogh's Ear,* and has poems in recent or forthcoming editions of *Verse, Slope, First Intensity,* and *New American Writing.*

www.ingramcontent.com/pod-product-compliance
Lightning Source LLC
Chambersburg PA
CBHW031857090426
42741CB00005B/535